HOW TO LOOK AFTER YOUR PET

KITTEN

KITTEN

Mark Evans

B.Vet.Med.

DK

DORLING KINDERSLEY

**LONDON, NEW YORK, MUNICH, PARIS,
MELBOURNE AND DELHI**

A DORLING KINDERSLEY BOOK

www.dk.com

For Mum and Dad

Project Editor Liza Bruml
Art Editor Jane Coney
Editor Miriam Farbey
Designer Rebecca Johns
Photographer Paul Bricknell
Illustrators Sally Hynard and Peter Visscher

Published in Great Britain by
Dorling Kindersley Limited
A Penguin Company
80 Strand, London, WC2R 0RL

10 9 8 7 6

A CIP catalogue record for this book
is available from the British Library.

ISBN 0-7513-5403-1

Colour reproduction by Colourscan, Singapore
Printed and bound in Spain by Artes Gráficas Toledo, S.A.
D.L. TO: 147-2002

Models: Narada Bernard, Jacob Brubert, Martin Cooles,
Louisa Hall, Corinne Hogarth, Thanh Huynh, Gupreet Janday,
Jason Kerim, Nathalie Lyon, Rachel Mamauag, Paul Mitchell,
Florence Prowen, Isabel Prowen, Jamie Sallon,
Maia Terry, Lisa Wardropper

Dorling Kindersley would like to thank everyone who allowed
us to photograph their pet, Jane Burton and Wood Green
Animal Shelters for providing cats, Christopher Howson for
design help, Bridget Hopkinson and Louise Pritchard
for editorial help and Lynn Bresler for the index.

Picture credits: Jane Burton p28 b, p29 cr, p35 cr, p40 tr, b,
p41 tl, cl, bl, br; Dave King p17 bc; NHPA/Stephen Dalton
p12 tr; NHPA/Manfred Danegger p13 tl; NHPA/Gerard Lacz
p16 tc, p17 br; Steve Shott p34 tr

Note to parents

This book teaches your child how to be
a caring and responsible pet owner. But
remember, your child must have your
help and guidance in every aspect of
day-to-day pet care. Don't let your child
have a cat unless you are sure that your
family has the time and resources
to look after it properly – for the
whole of its life.

Contents

Introduction

The first step to becoming a good cat owner is to choose the right sort of cat. It is how a cat behaves that is most important, not what she looks like or how old she is. She is going to be your best friend. You will spend a lot of time playing together. But remember, you need to look after her every day. Not just to start with, but for the whole of her life.

You will need to buy special things for your cat

Understanding your pet

By watching your cat carefully, you will learn her special way of talking. From a flick of her tail, or the movement of her ears, you will see if she is happy or sad. And you will soon understand what she is saying when she miaows or purrs.

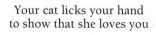

Your cat licks your hand to show that she loves you

Caring for your pet

You will only be your cat's best friend if you care for her properly. You will need to make sure that she eats the right foods, always has water, and can get plenty of exercise every day. You will also have to groom her often, and spend some time training her.

You will need to groom your cat every day

Things to do with your pet

Your cat loves to play with toys. She likes chasing and pouncing games the best. These help her practise her hunting skills.

Your kitten will bat a dangling toy

People to help

The best cat owner always tries to find out more about her pet. You can ask your vet and nurse any questions you have about how to keep your pet healthy.

You will need to visit your vet centre regularly

New family member

Your cat is a very independent animal. But if you care for her properly, she will enjoy being part of your family. She can even make a good friend for some of your other pets. You can train her to obey the rules you and your family make for her.

Things to remember:
When you live with a pet cat, there are some important rules you must always follow:

🐾 Wash your hands after stroking or playing with your cat.

🐾 Never allow your cat to eat food from your plate.

🐾 Don't let your cat on the kitchen units or the dinner table.

🐾 Don't let your cat on your bed.

🐾 If your cat is fast asleep, don't wake her up suddenly.

🐾 Never, ever tease or hit your cat.

Ask a grown-up
👫 When you see this sign in the book, you should ask an adult to help you.

Your cat will become part of your family

What is a cat?

Cats belong to a group of animals called mammals. Like all mammals, cats have warm blood and a furry body. When they are young, they drink milk from their mothers. Not all cats look the same. They can be big or small, long-haired or short-haired. As they grow up, they develop keen senses and supple, athletic bodies.

Ear can turn in every direction to pick up sounds

Narrow shoulders allow cat to slip through small spaces

Life on four legs
Every part of your cat's body does its own job. His fur coat helps keep him warm. His slender body lets him squeeze through tiny gaps and twist around obstacles. Strong muscles power his hind legs so he can jump a long way and run fast over short distances. His long tail helps him to balance.

Thick fur helps keep cat warm

Pink nipple

Rough, pink paw pads give good grip

Flat tummy button is hidden by fur

Underneath your cat
Look closely at your cat's tummy and you will find that she has a flat tummy button. Count the nipples. You will usually find eight. In a mother cat, they are sucked for milk by her young kittens.

Claws are kept in a skin pocket called a sheath

Ear perks
up to listen

Pupil becomes
small slit in
bright light

Moist nose
detects smells

Whiskers feel in
the dark to help
him find his way

Long tail swings
from side to side
for balance

Upright
tail shows
cat is alert

Super senses

Your cat has better senses than you. He sees
more clearly than you in dim light. He hears
faint sounds when you think it is quiet. He
can even tell if other cats have been about
by sniffing for their special scents.

Heel is a long way
off the ground – this
helps him run faster

Back leg is large
and strong

Four-toed
back paw has
sharp claws

He always
stands on tiptoes

Look closer at your cat

Pointed teeth, called
canines, are used
to hold food

Black pupils change
shape depending on
the amount of light

Hook-like front
claws come out of
sheaths for grasping

Five-toed front paws
have rough pads for
protection

Tiny spines on
tongue strip meat off
bones and pick out
dirt from fur

11

Life in the wild

Pet cats are members of the felid family. Wild members of this family include big cats like the tiger, and small cats like the puma. Wild cats usually like to live on their own. A very long time ago, small wild cats began to kill the mice and rats that ate people's grain. The people cared for the most friendly cats and they soon became pets.

European wild cat

Always wild

The European wild cat, like many small wild cats, is very shy. Even though it looks like a pet cat, it is so timid that it can never live with people. But the North African wild cat is bolder. It is thought to be the ancestor of the pet cat.

Feral long-haired cat has dirty, matted fur

Brave cat crouches, ready to pounce

Cat sits and watches all the other alley cats

Tough cat stares meanly

Old cat lies down but keeps a sharp lookout

Lioness stays close to the young cubs

Pride of lions

Some big cats, such as the lion, live together in a family pack, called a pride. There may be as many as twenty lions in a pride. Together, they hunt and kill wild animals for food.

Your parents will help you decide the rules for your cat

Alley cats

Pet cats living wild in cities and on farms are called feral cats. They often live in groups. They hunt small animals for food and eat waste scraps. When there is not enough food, some cats leave the group. The cats that stay together may fight over food.

Alert cat has tail in the air

Kitten looks for someone to play with

New friends

People make good friends for cats. You never fight for food with your pet cats. You feed them, give them a warm place to sleep and keep their coats tidy. Although most cats are independent, they will enjoy being part of the family.

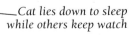
Cat lies down to sleep while others keep watch

Types of cat

Many years ago, some people began to decide which cats should have kittens. They chose the cats with unusual features, such as long hair, or beautiful coat colours. Many types, or breeds, of cat with different looks were produced. Some cats, called mongrels, are a mixture of breeds.

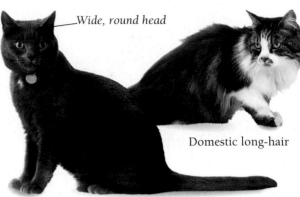

Wide, round head

Domestic long-hair

Domestic short-hair

Domestic cats

The most common type of cat is called a domestic. All domestics are crossbreds, or mongrels. Domestics have large, broad heads. Some have long hair, others have short, sleek coats.

Siamese

Siamese cats have short fur, a lean body and a pointed head. They are very friendly and miaow very often.

Large, pointed ears

Smooth, sleek coat

Siamese

Persian

Persian cats have very long and woolly coats. They have round, flat faces and stocky bodies. They are often not as friendly or playful as other cats.

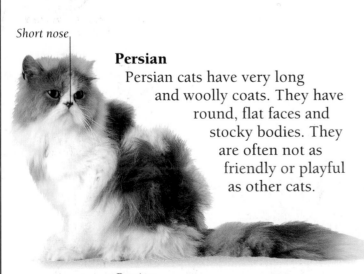

Short nose

Persian

Fine coat dries quickly

Turkish Van

Turkish Van

Turkish Van cats have very silky coats. Unlike other cats, they love to play in water. They are often called Turkish swimming cats.

Dark brown diamond patch on face

Fur is thick and silky

Ragdoll

Coat is sleek and glossy

Burmese

Ragdoll
Large and gentle Ragdoll cats look like Birmans. But if you pick them up, they will hang limply – like a ragdoll!

Maine Coon

Maine Coon
Big, strong Maine Coon cats have shaggy coats. They make loving pets.

Burmese
Although closely related to Siamese cats, Burmese cats have rounder faces. They are very active and love people.

Birman
Lively Birman cats enjoy company. They may look like Siameses, but they have longer coats.

Birman

Long and fluffy tail

Fur is very long on chest and tummy

Abyssinian
Beautiful Abyssinians are very slender, with long, thin legs and big ears. They are alert and clever, and often make a lot of noise.

Short, dense fur

Abyssinian mother and kittens

From purebred to mongrel

Two purebreds have another purebred

Purebred looks the same as its parents

Different purebreds have a crossbred

A crossbred is a mixture of its parents

Two crossbreds have a mongrel cat

Every mongrel cat looks slightly different

15

Selecting for looks

All cats have the same parts – a head with eyes, ears, mouth and nose, and a body with a furry coat. The size, shape and colour of these parts is different in every cat. But don't be tempted to choose a cat just for her looks. Look at the way she behaves as well. After all, you are choosing a friend for life.

Scottish Fold

Domestic short-hair

Burmese

Maine Coon

Domestic short-hair

Persian

Head shapes

Most cats have a round head with a wide face. Persian cats have a broad head and a very flat face. Other cats have a narrow head with a pointed face.

Tonkinese

Big or small ears?

Cats can have all kinds of ears. Mongrel cats mostly have small, pointed ears. Cats that first came from hot countries often have large ears. Some cats have hairy ears, while other cats' ears are even folded!

Coat colours

A cat's coat may be all one colour, such as black, white or chocolate. Some coats are a mixture of two or more colours. When a cat is ginger and black, it is called a tortoiseshell.

Tortoiseshell tail

White back

Black fur

Black back

White leg

Bi-coloured coat

Tri-coloured coat

Plain coat

Coat patterns

Cats may have a spotty pattern all over their coats. Other cats, called tabby, have a stripy coat. Many cats have blotchy coats. When dark patches are on the ears, face, paws and tail, they are called "points".

Black spots

Dark spots ring tail

Tabby pattern on back with white patch

"Points" on ears

Ocicat

Dark tail

Siamese

Brown paws

Domestic short-hair

White paws

Long hair is soft

Short coat is smooth

Ragdoll

Domestic tabby and white

Hairstyles for cats

Fur can be many different lengths. Most pet cats have short hair. It is easy to clean, and it does not get knotted. Long-haired cats have silky coats that can tangle. Their fur must be brushed every day.

No whiskers

Hairless skin is wrinkly

Extraordinary and strange

Some cats have very unusual features. Manx cats look like ordinary cats, but have no tails! Polydactyl cats are born with too many toes. Instead of five on each front paw, they have as many as seven. The weirdest cat is the Sphynx. It is almost bald.

Cat has stump where tail should start

Polydactyl

Kitten has seven toes

Manx

Sphynx

Things to get ready

You will need to get some special equipment for your new pet. All the items should be well made. Make sure everything is ready before you fetch your kitten. As a kitten tries to play with almost anything, check that nothing dangerous is left out.

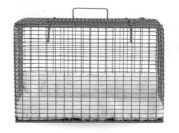
Wire cage

Plastic carrying box

Carrying baskets
You need a basket in which to carry your kitten. Ask your vet for a special carrying box. A strong wire cage will last longer.

Covered bed

Cosy bed
Your kitten will sleep in all sorts of places. She will also like to curl up in her soft, warm cat bed.

Feeding equipment
Buy a water bowl, a food bowl and a plastic container in which to store dried food. To serve up the food, get your cat her own spoon and fork.

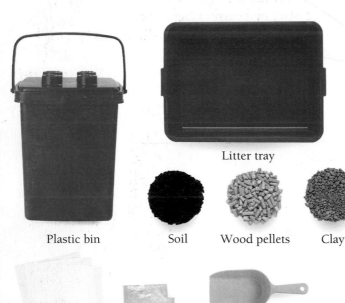
Litter tray

Plastic bin   Soil   Wood pellets   Clay

Paper   Litter tray liners

Scoop

Shovel

Litter tray and litter
Cats that live indoors, and all kittens, go to the toilet in a litter tray. Buy a plastic litter tray and litter liners. You will need some litter, a scoop to fill the tray, and a shovel to clean and empty it. You can keep litter fresh in a storage bin. Find some old paper to put under the tray to keep the floor clean.

Airtight container

Spoon

Fork

Water bowl

Food bowl

Collar

Nylon collar

Buy a collar with elastic in it. If the collar gets caught, the elastic will stretch. Your cat can pull her head through to escape.

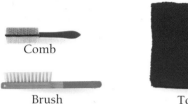

Comb

Brush

Towel

Gooming equipment

Buy your cat a fine comb and a soft brush. Your cat should also have her own towel for you to dry her with.

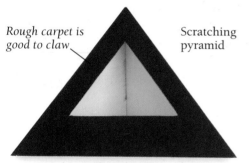

Rough carpet is good to claw

Scratching pyramid

Scratching pyramid

Your cat will want to scratch with her claws. Buy or make a scratching post so she doesn't scratch the furniture.

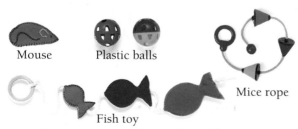

Mouse

Plastic balls

Mice rope

Fish toy

Cat toys

Cats love to play with things that move or make a noise. Buy or make some strong, small toys for your cat.

Identity disc

Buy an identity disc to attach to your cat's collar. Have your address and phone number engraved on it.

Metal identity disc

Flap can be pushed open by cat's head

Cat-flap

Your cat likes to get in and out of your house whenever she wants. Buy a clear cat-flap to put in your door.

Bucket

Rubber gloves

Scrubbing brush

Disinfectant

Odour remover

Squeaky clean

Your cat will sometimes make a mess. You will need some special cleaning things to clean up after her. Always wear the rubber gloves when cleaning.

Danger!

Some things hurt cats.

Trailing cables are dangerous

Wool and needles can be swallowed

Some indoor and garden plants are poisonous

Cleaning fluids and chemicals harm your cat

Cats like warm places, but hot things can burn

Rubbish may choke your cat

Choosing your cat

You can choose a kitten from a litter when she is around four weeks old. You can't take her home until she is six weeks old, and ready to leave her mother. Meet the mother cat, so you can see what your kitten will be like when she is fully grown. Make sure the kitten is healthy.

Kitten watches dangling toy

Cuddly kitten

Before you get an adorable kitten, think carefully. You will be kept very busy playing with him and keeping him out of trouble.

Old and wise

A grown-up cat can be as friendly as a kitten, but he is more independent.

Where to find your new pet

* A friend's cat may have a litter.
* A breeder will sell you a purebred.
* An animal shelter has cats of all ages and kinds that need a new home.

Curious kitten

Noisy kitten

Shy kitten

1 When the owner takes you to see the litter, watch from a place where the kittens can't see you. Look for a lively kitten that likes to play with her sisters and brothers, but is not a bully.

2 Say hello to the kittens' mother. See if she is friendly. She should start to purr when you stroke her.

Stroke the mother cat

Kitten stays close to her mother

3 **Watch the kittens** to see which one is the friendliest. They will think you are a climbing frame and clamber all over you. Pick out the one you like.

Kitten cuddles up to you

4 **Ask the owner** how to pick up your favourite kitten. Find out what sex it is. Check the kitten is healthy. She must have bright eyes and a clean nose. Her mouth should be pale pink, with tiny, white teeth. Check that her coat is clean all over, even under her tail.

Paperwork
Write down the food, medicines and injections your cat has been given. Your vet will want to know.

Check that each ear is clean

Hold up the kitten to have a good look

Two fingers should fit under collar

5 **Go back to collect** your kitten when she is at least six weeks old. Take with you the collar and identity disc, and a carrying box to put your kitten in on the journey home.

Fold-up carrying box

❖ Boy or girl?
Boy cats are usually bigger than girls. They wander farther from home and may get into more fights. You should get your cat neutered when he or she is about six months old (see p40).

Welcome home

To help your kitten settle in quickly, get everything ready before she arrives. Put her in one room for the first few days. Make sure that all the windows are shut. After this, she can explore the whole house. She must always be able to get to her bed.

Female cat

Male cat

Visiting your vet

Arrange to visit your vet on the way home from collecting your new kitten. The vet will check your pet all over to make sure she is healthy. He will also tell you if she needs any injections.

What sex is your kitten?

When a kitten is very young, it can be hard to tell if it is a male or a female. Ask your vet to check the sex.

How to pick up your kitten

You will want to pick your kitten up to cuddle her or to stop her getting into trouble! Put one hand under her back legs. Put the other hand around her tummy and then lift her. If she starts to wriggle, put her down again gently.

Put one hand gently around her chest

Put one hand under her back legs

Meeting a dog

Your cat and your dog can become best friends. Let them meet as soon as your cat has settled in. Watch them carefully to make sure they don't fight.

Sniffing the new family member

Cat stares at dog

Kitten turns away as he is timid

Cat stares at stranger

Meeting another cat

If you already have one cat, let your new pet get to know it slowly. Don't leave the cats alone together. If your kitten is too playful, the other cat may swipe at him.

Preparing the litter tray

Put the filled litter tray in a quiet corner of the room. Your kitten does not like to eat or sleep near her toilet.

Storage bin full of litter

Fill the litter tray

A cosy corner

Choose a warm corner of the room for your kitten's bed and eating area. Always put down a bowl of water for your kitten. You can also leave her some dry food (see p24).

Dangle rope toy for kitten to bat

Cover over bed makes kitten feel safe

Warm bed

23

Feeding your cat

Your cat is a carnivore, or meat-eater, but she may eat small amounts of plants and vegetables too. To keep your cat healthy, it is best to buy food specially made for cats. You can choose between moist or dry food. Ask your vet to help you choose the right food for your cat.

The carnivore
If your cat doesn't eat meat she will become very ill. She uses her pointed canine teeth to grip the meat.

Your cat eats crouching down

"Complete"
dry food

"Complete"
moist food

Side teeth shear
Your cat's razor-sharp side teeth chop food up into pieces small enough to swallow.

All-in-one
The simplest way to feed your cat is with a "complete" food. It contains all the things he needs. The food is either moist or dry. Cats love to crunch dry food.

Dry biscuit

Moist food

"Complementary" food

Mixing foods
"Complementary" food must be served with another food to make a healthy meal.

Look for the word "cat"

"Complete" food needs nothing added

Buying the food
👫 Carefully read the writing on the packet. Make sure that the food is for cats, and contains meat. This label is from a food for adult cats. A kitten needs a food for growing cats.

CAT FOOD

Fully tested

Food is for cats over one year old. It is a complete pet food.

Feed as much food as your cat will eat in at least two meals a day.

Ingredients: meat and fats
Protein ~%, Oil ~%, Fibre ~%, Water ~%, Vitamins A, D, E
Always leave fresh water

Best before

grams

Look for the word "tested"

Recycling sign

Use by date

Weight

Bar code

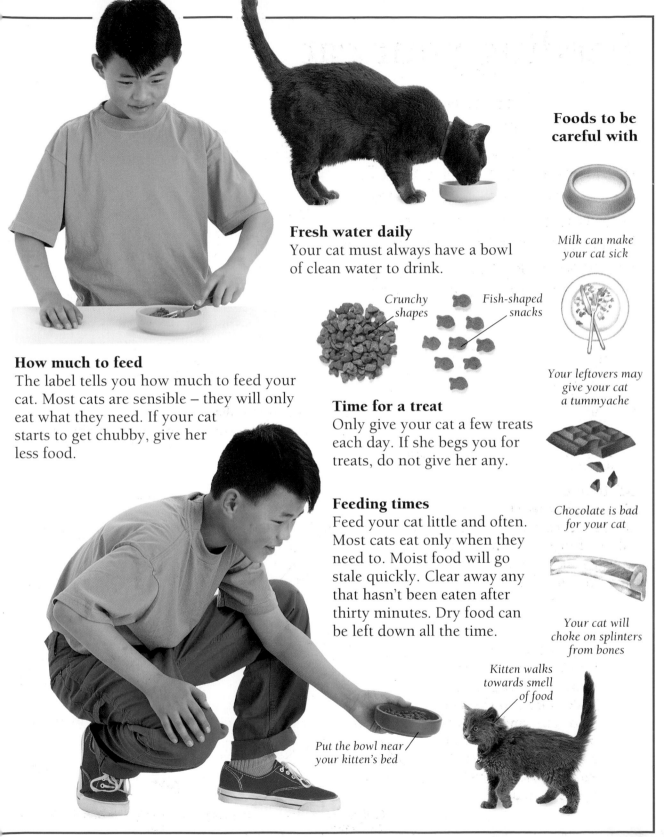

Foods to be careful with

Milk can make your cat sick

Your leftovers may give your cat a tummyache

Chocolate is bad for your cat

Your cat will choke on splinters from bones

Fresh water daily

Your cat must always have a bowl of clean water to drink.

Crunchy shapes

Fish-shaped snacks

Time for a treat

Only give your cat a few treats each day. If she begs you for treats, do not give her any.

How much to feed

The label tells you how much to feed your cat. Most cats are sensible – they will only eat what they need. If your cat starts to get chubby, give her less food.

Feeding times

Feed your cat little and often. Most cats eat only when they need to. Moist food will go stale quickly. Clear away any that hasn't been eaten after thirty minutes. Dry food can be left down all the time.

Kitten walks towards smell of food

Put the bowl near your kitten's bed

The happy cat

A pet cat can tell you in a lot of ways that he is happy. He doesn't smile and laugh, or talk to you by using words. Instead, he makes a few different noises. Listen carefully, and you will often hear him purring or chirping. He also does certain things to show you that he is content. You will see him playing and sleeping, and feel him brushing against you. You will soon learn to recognise a happy cat.

Cat licks paw to wipe his face

Grooming when relaxed
Your cat may wash himself when he is content, even if he is clean. Sometimes he grooms himself if he is worried, to calm himself down.

The head rub
Your cat's way of greeting you is to rub against you. This is his own way of saying hello. He tries to get as close to you as possible.

Tail up shows cat is interested

Head brushes against your sleeve to give a "head rub"

Cat hears a noise and looks around

Dozy cat lies down

Cat-napping
When cats are completely relaxed, they will become dozy. They half-shut their eyes. If something disturbs them, they will get up and have a look.

Marking a friend

If a cat likes you, she makes sure that she will recognise you next time you meet. She rubs her body against you and curls her tail around your legs to mark you with her invisible scent.

Cat wraps herself around your legs to leave her scent

Happy cat wrestles with his favourite toy

Purring with pleasure

You can tell that your cat is happy when you see him play. You will sometimes hear him make a rumbling sound, or purr, when he is content.

Your lap is a comfortable, warm seat

Rough tongue tickles

Sitting comfortably

On your lap, your cat may lick you to wash your skin. He may also push his claws into your legs. He doesn't mean to hurt you – he's saying that he loves you.

Cat talk

You will hear when your cat is pleased. She may purr, chirp or miaow. Try and work out exactly what she is trying to say to you.

Siamese cat is pleased to see you

Happy miaow

The frightened cat

Your cat is quite cowardly. If something frightens him he may run and hide. He doesn't like to fight. If another cat tries to come into his territory, he pretends that he is brave. He puffs himself up very large, using every part of his body to give off "go away" signals. If the enemy doesn't leave, your cat may get angry. He may roll over and show his claws and teeth. You will hear him hiss.

What frightens your cat?

Firework bangs terrify cats

Strange dogs may threaten your cat

Some cats hate to travel

Trying to look brave

Sometimes you will see your cat look very different. All his hair stands on end, and his back arches. The pupils in his eyes change from slits to circles. Your cat is scared. He is making himself as large as he can to frighten away whatever is scaring him.

Calming down your cat
- Switch off the lights.
- Talk in a soothing voice.
- Give your cat some food.
- Remove the thing that is scaring him.

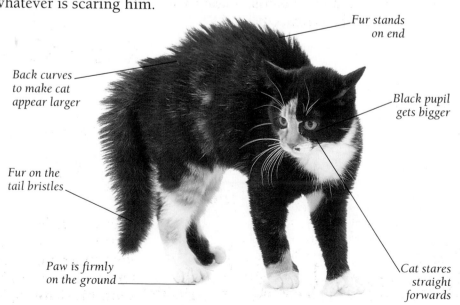

Fur stands on end

Back curves to make cat appear larger

Black pupil gets bigger

Fur on the tail bristles

Paw is firmly on the ground

Cat stares straight forwards

Escaping from danger

Cats usually like to run away when they are upset. Your cat may crawl under your bed, or jump up onto a shelf. He likes to sit and watch from a high place where nothing can reach him.

Cat has fled to safety on top shelf

Growling in anger

When your cat is not scared, but very annoyed, she crouches down. She makes a low, grumbling sound, and stares at whatever is upsetting her without blinking. The dark pupils in her eyes become slits. It is best to leave your cat alone when she is irritated.

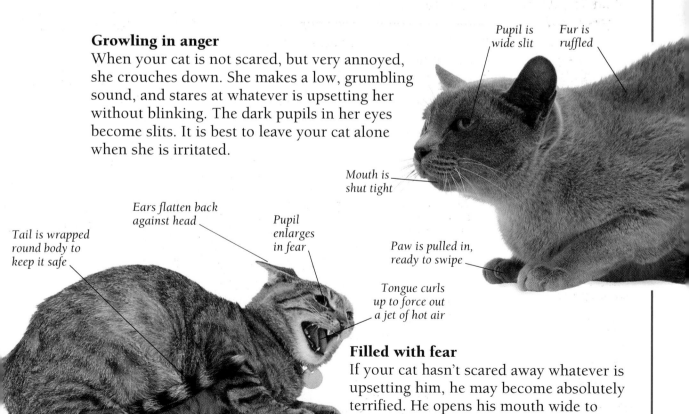

Pupil is wide slit

Fur is ruffled

Mouth is shut tight

Ears flatten back against head

Pupil enlarges in fear

Tail is wrapped round body to keep it safe

Paw is pulled in, ready to swipe

Tongue curls up to force out a jet of hot air

Filled with fear

If your cat hasn't scared away whatever is upsetting him, he may become absolutely terrified. He opens his mouth wide to show his sharp teeth and hisses loudly.

Training your cat

You will not be able to train your cat to sit or stay like a dog. But you can teach her things like her name, where to go to the toilet, and how to use a cat-flap. And she may surprise you with the things that she teaches herself to do.

Mother cat using her litter tray

Kittens watch their mother

Learning from mother
Young kittens watch their mother go to the toilet in a litter tray. They quickly learn that when they want to go, they should also use the tray.

Toilet training your pet
Every half an hour, when your kitten is awake, gently lift him into the tray. Your kitten will prefer to have his tray in a quiet corner of the room, away from his food.

Carefully lift your kitten into his litter tray

Tray filled with fresh litter

Litter liner

Keeping the tray clean
When your kitten has been to the toilet, scoop out the litter that was used. He won't use dirty litter. At the end of every day, clean and re-fill the tray.

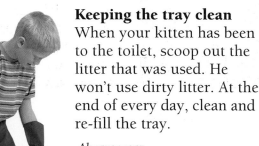

Always wear rubber gloves

Remove used litter with the shovel

Accidents will happen!
All young kittens have accidents. You must clean up the mess. Scrub the floor with water and disinfectant. Then spray it with odour remover. If your kitten can smell the mess, he will probably have another accident in the same spot.

Odour remover

Wear your gloves

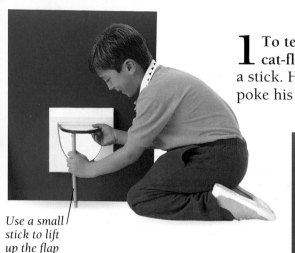

1 To teach your cat how to use the cat-flap, prop the flap open with a stick. He will discover that he can poke his head out to look around.

Use a small stick to lift up the flap

2 Next tempt your cat through the flap door. Open the flap slightly and show him some food. He will nudge the flap open with his head, and then climb through.

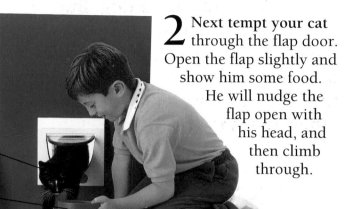

Cat climbs through the flap carefully

Hold out a bowl of food as a reward

3 Leave the cat-flap unlocked during the day. Your cat will learn quickly how to use the flap without your help. He will soon come and go as he likes.

Cat darts out of flap

How to reward a good cat
🐾 Give him a big cuddle.
🐾 Play a game with him.
🐾 Give him a food treat.

Telling off your cat
If you catch your cat being naughty, say "No" sharply. Never smack him. If you do, he will think twice before coming near you again.

Fair punishment
You can scare your cat away from doing something naughty.

Point your finger at the naughty cat

Bad cat tries to eat plant

Spray your cat with a little water. He hates to be wet

Loud noises frighten your cat

Indoor cat

Cats spend a lot of time indoors. They like to find the warmest places to curl up and go to sleep, which won't always be in their beds. Your cat may not be able to go outside. But there are many different things that she can do indoors to keep active and fit.

A cardboard house is fun to hide in

Lookout platform

Swing the ball toy for your cat to swipe

Rough rope gives good grip for climbing

Adventure playground
You can make or buy an indoor activity centre for your cat. It's a climbing frame, a scratching post and a play area rolled into one. It should be sturdy, as cats hate walking on things that wobble.

Cat peeps out of tube

Fur-lined tube makes a cosy, warm bed

Be ready to lift up the rope

Scratching post

Your cat needs to keep his claws trimmed. Buy a scratching post or make one using rope. This should stop your cat damaging furniture.

Cat rasps claws against carpet

Cardboard pyramid covered in carpet

Indoor games

Play "hunting" games with your cat. Dangle a soft toy in front of her. Pull it away quickly when she tries to grab it. She'll be much quicker than you.

Cat holds on to the toy with front paws

Furry cover keeps the cradle warm

Beware!

Cats may sleep in dangerous places.

Keep the washing machine door shut

Cat cradle

Your cat loves to lounge in a cradle hanging over a radiator. She will keep a lookout from this snug bed.

Make sure your cat can't climb into the car

Your cat may prefer a bed without a roof

Keep a guard over the fireplace

Cat curls up in basket

Time for bed

See where your cat most likes to sleep. Put his proper bed there. He will probably change his favourite place after a while.

Strange sleeping places

Sometimes you will find your cat sleeping in the most unlikely places. So keep on looking if you think he is lost!

Outdoor cat

Cats can go outside a week after they have had their injections (see p22). Your cat may stay in the garden, but he may explore your neighbourhood. He practises hunting skills and marks out the area that belongs to him. He scratches and rubs against things to leave his scent. He makes regular patrols of his territory and may fight invading cats (see p28).

Learning to hunt

Watch your cat creep up, wait for the right moment, and then pounce on leaves blowing in the wind. She is practising her hunting skills.

Cat stalks rustling leaves

Paw ready to swipe

Cat creeps along fence

The athlete

Cats have an excellent sense of balance. They hardly ever fall from high places. They can run along very narrow ledges without fear of slipping. When cats jump, they crouch, and then spring into the air by suddenly straightening their strong back legs.

Front feet first

When cats jump down, they almost always land on their feet. The pads that are on their front paws cushion their landing.

Hind legs are tucked in

Front legs absorb shock

Climbing high

Your cat likes to keep watch from the highest place he can climb to. He uses his hooked claws to pull himself up a tree. He either scrambles or jumps down.

Cat stares down at you

A private place to toilet in

Male and female cats dig a hole where they want to toilet

They squat over the hole. Most cats bury their droppings

Cats may stand and spray urine to mark out their territory

Beckoning will encourage your cat to come down if he is stuck

Cat sharpens his claws on the bark

Scratching bark

A tree trunk makes a good scratching post for your cat. The fine scratch marks are messages. They tell other cats that the tree is in your cat's territory.

Cat stands up on back legs to scratch

Leaving special scent

You will often see your cat rub her body against things in the garden to leave her unique scent. Other cats can tell from the scent whether your cat is male or female, and how long ago she was there.

Cat's side rubs against plant to leave her smell

35

Good grooming

Your cat is covered in fur from his nose to the tip of his tail. There are times when your cat sheds a lot of hair, or moults. He licks his coat regularly to make sure it stays clean, and to remove any loose hairs. Groom your cat every day. This keeps his coat in good condition and helps him get used to being handled.

Paw is licked to wash face

Face washing
Your cat has a clever way of washing his face. He uses his saliva instead of soap and water, and his paw as a flannel. He wipes his paw in circles around his cheeks. Then he reaches to wash behind his ears.

Head twists around to reach

Front teeth nibble away any dirt

Removing bits of dirt
Dirt and tiny twigs get caught in your cat's fur. The fur also gets knotted. Your cat uses his small front teeth to pick out the dirt and untangle knots of hair.

Back curves to let cat groom leg

Leg stretches up into the air

Rough tongue licks inside leg

🐾 Fur balls
Your cat swallows the loose hair that he pulls out when he grooms himself. The fur usually passes straight out of him. Long-haired and moulting cats may swallow too much fur. The hair sometimes rolls into a small ball in his tummy. If your cat coughs up fur balls, contact your vet.

Bending to lick all over
The surface of your cat's tongue is covered in hard, little prongs. He uses it like a comb. His body is very flexible, so he can reach to groom almost every part of it.

Brushing a long-haired cat

Begin to groom your cat by brushing his back. Brush the coat from the head towards the tail. Your cat loves to feel the brush strokes on his back – he may even start to purr.

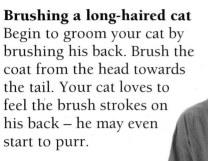

Cradle the cat in your lap

Happy cat starts to purr

Combing the hair

When you have brushed the coat, gently pull the comb through the hair. Don't be too rough. If you find a knot, untangle it with your fingers. Make sure you comb the whole coat, especially the tummy.

Comb one section of the coat at a time

Brushing short hair

Give your short-haired cat a quick brush all over every day. While you are brushing her, you can check the condition of her coat (see p42).

Brush her back first

Drying a wet cat

If your cat gets very wet, dry him with his own towel. Sit him between your knees and rub his coat all over. His paw pads may be muddy, so don't forget to wipe them.

Wrap the towel around your cat

Your kitten grows up

You and your cat are a team for life. You will have to care for him every day of the year. When he is a kitten you will have to look after him just like his mother did. By the time he is a year old, he will be grown up. He will do many things on his own but he will still like your company. Your cat will live a long time. When he is old, he will need special care.

Eye of very young kitten still closed

Caring for a kitten
A young kitten is helpless. He needs his mother to give him food and to clean up after him. His mother teaches him how to groom himself, hunt for food and use a litter tray.

Playing games
When kittens are a few weeks old, they begin to play with each other. They learn all the skills they will need when they are older. By the time kittens are 14 weeks old, they are as agile and graceful as adult cats.

Kitten play fights to practise his hunting skills

Rosette for the winning owner

Groomed coat

Prize-winning Ragdoll cat

Carefree as a kitten
A grown-up cat knows she can rely on you to give her food and a warm bed. She can spend time playing with you as she doesn't have to hunt for food.

Cat uses her tail to help her balance

Showing your cat
You can take your cat to a cat show. The judge will give prizes to the cats that are the best examples of their type, or breed. At other kinds of shows, your cat could win a prize for having the loudest purr or the bushiest tail!

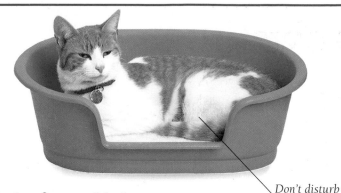

Don't disturb a sleeping or resting old cat

Caring for an elderly cat

When your cat is older, he will want to sleep more. He may find it difficult to reach to wash his coat, so he will need more help with grooming. Take him to the vet for regular check-ups.

Shake the rope so toy mice move

Paws grip toy mouse

Cat stands to reach toy

Leaving your cat

Away from your pet
You can't always take your cat with you everywhere you go. You will have to leave him for a few hours while you are at school, and when you go on holiday.

Out for a short time
Before you leave, make sure your pet has some food, fresh water, toys and a clean litter tray. If you are happy for your cat to go outdoors, check that the cat-flap is unlocked.

Looked after by friends
When you go on holiday, your cat prefers to stay at home. Try to find a friend who is able to look after your pet every day. Write down a list of the daily jobs that need to be done, and the name and telephone number of your vet.

The cattery
If no one can come to your home to look after your cat, you can put your pet in a cattery. This is like a hotel for cats. Whenever you travel with your cat, put him in a strong carrying basket.

Neutering your kitten

Just as women can have children, female cats can have kittens. There may be as many as eight kittens in a litter. You should think carefully about whether you want your cat to have kittens. Your vet can give both female and male cats an operation that is called neutering. After it, your cat won't be able to have kittens.

🐾 Responsible ownership

You may think it is fun for your female cat to have kittens. But it is usually best to have your cat neutered. Letting your cat have kittens can be very expensive. You need to do a lot of planning, and you have to find a good home for each one of the kittens.

The same but different
Your cat will look almost the same after a neutering operation as he or she did before it. But your cat will act differently. A male cat that is neutered does not look for a girlfriend, or have so many fights. A neutered female cat does not worry about kittens.

You won't feel any difference

1 **Newborn kittens** can sleep, drink and crawl. They suck their mother's nipples for some milk. The mother cat spends a lot of time looking after her kittens. She licks them to keep them clean.

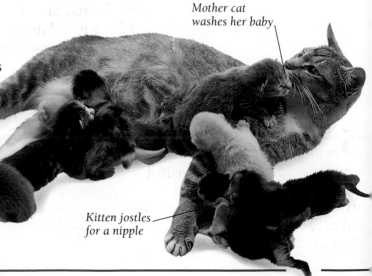

Mother cat washes her baby

Mother stretches out leg to let kittens reach her nipples

Kitten jostles for a nipple

Eye is closed

Keen nose guides kitten to mother

2 **A four-day-old kitten** still cannot see or hear. He can crawl, but is very wobbly when he tries to stand up. By the time he is ten days old, his eyes will have opened and he will hear his first sounds.

3 **When a kitten is four weeks old,** he has learnt to walk. He likes to play games with the other kittens in the litter and with his owner. In a few weeks time, he will be ready to leave his mother, and go to a new home.

Play with your kitten so that he gets used to you

Tail raised for balance

Ear listens for the noise of the toy

Kitten has learnt to walk on tiptoes

4 **At five months old,** a kitten starts to be less playful. He is growing up quickly and may start to fight other cats. In a month's time, he and his sisters will be able to have kittens. It will be time to have them neutered.

Ear is forward as cat is alert

5 **After about a year,** your kitten will be a grown-up cat. He is very independent. He will patrol his territory regularly. If his sisters were not neutered, they could already have mothered a litter of kittens of their own.

Health care

You need to look after your cat properly to make sure that she stays fit and healthy. You should give her the right food (see p24), keep her well groomed (p36), and do several quick and simple health checks. If you do these every day, you will learn to spot quickly if your cat is unwell. If you think something is wrong, take her to your vet straight away.

Healthy coat looks glossy

Push fur backwards

1 **Check that your cat's coat** is in good condition. Run your fingers through her fur. It should feel dry, and smell clean. Do not forget to check hidden places, like under her tail.

Claw is the right length

Claw is too long

Use one arm to hold your cat around her middle

2 **Look carefully at your cat's paws.** Check that nothing is stuck in her pads or in the fur between her toes. Gently squeeze each paw so her claws come out. Make sure that they are clean and not too long.

Gently pull back the flap

3 **Examine your cat's ears.** Hold back the pointed part of each ear in turn and look down the hairy hole. The ear should be clean. If it smells, your cat may be ill.

4 Check your cat's eyes. A bright light will help you see them clearly. Put one hand under her chin, and the other on top of her head. Her eyes should be bright and shiny, with no tears in the corners.

Keep her head still

5 🏃🏃 Make sure nothing is stuck in your cat's mouth. Put one hand over her nose and tip her head back. Her mouth will start to open. Use your other hand to pull her jaw down. Her tongue should be pink.

Teeth should be clean and white

Pet toothpaste

Long-handled toothbrush

6 🏃🏃 Brush your cat's teeth every day. Put some pet toothpaste on your cat's toothbrush. Put the brush in the side of her mouth. Brush backwards and forwards along the outside of the teeth.

Use the small end of the brush

Hold your cat's jaw firmly

Your pet care check list

Use this list to keep a record of all the jobs you need to do.

Copy this chart. Tick off the jobs when you have finished them

Every day:

Feed your cat

Clean bowls

Put down fresh water

Scoop out used litter

Groom coat

Check fur

Examine paws

Check ears and eyes

Look inside mouth

Clean teeth

Wash litter tray

◆

Once a week:

Weigh your cat

Tidy activity centre

Check the food and litter supplies

◆

Once a month:

Give medicines

Wash fur blanket

◆

Every year:

Take your cat to the vet for a check-up

Injections

Visiting your vet centre

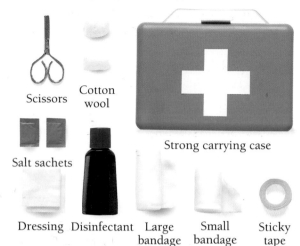

The vets and the nurses who work at your local vet centre want to keep your cat healthy and happy. They will tell you how to look after your cat properly. You can ask them as many questions as you like. They will also try to make your cat better if he is ill.

Scissors

Cotton wool

Strong carrying case

Salt sachets

Dressing Disinfectant Large bandage Small bandage Sticky tape

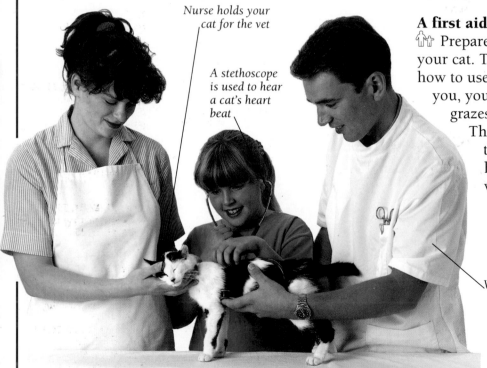

Nurse holds your cat for the vet

A stethoscope is used to hear a cat's heart beat

White coat keeps the vet clean

A first aid kit for cats

Prepare a special first aid kit for your cat. The nurse will explain how to use everything. Just like you, your cat sometimes cuts or grazes himself by accident. The kit contains all the things you need to make him feel better on the way to the vet centre.

Your vet's nurse

The nurse helps your vet. She knows a lot about cats. When you have any questions about your cat, visit or telephone the nurse at your vet centre.

Your vet

Your vet gives your cat special health checks. If your cat is ill, he will tell you what needs to be done to make him better. He may give you medicine for your cat.

My pet's fact sheet

Try making a fact sheet about your pet cat. Copy the headings on this page, or you can make up your own. Then write in the correct information about your cat.

Pointed ear

White chest

Long, black tail

White sock

Leave a space to stick in a photograph or draw a picture of your cat. Then label all of your pet's special features.

Name: Tess

Birthday: 21st August

Weight: 900 g (2 lb)

Type of food fed: Complete dry food

Best game: Fish toy

Vet's name: Mark Evans

Nurse's name: Rebecca Johns

Vet centre telephone number: 089582 2324

Medicines and injections

Your cat may be ill if tiny worms live inside him or insects crawl on his coat. To keep them away, the nurse will give you some special medicines for your cat. Germs can also make your cat sick. The vet will give your cat injections every year to help protect him from them.